T0097439

T HE N E W NI GHT
OF A LWAY S

P.O. Box 200340
Brooklyn, NY 11220
upsetpress.org

Copyright © 2016 by Robert Booras

All poems written by Robert Booras except
"The Poetry Group Tombstone," by Robert Booras & Nicholas Powers

All rights reserved. No part of this book may be reproduced, stored in a retrieval system, or transmitted in any form or by any means without the prior written permission of both the copyright owner and the above publisher of this book, except in the case of brief quotations embodied in critical articles or reviews.

Established in 2000, UpSet Press is an independent press based in Brooklyn. The original impetus of the press was to upset the status quo through literature. UpSet Press has expanded its mission to promote new work by new authors; the first works, or complete works, of established authors—placing a special emphasis on restoring to print new editions of exceptional texts; and first-time translations of works into English. Overall, UpSet Press endeavors to advance authors' innovative visions, and works that engender new directions in literature.

Robert Booras received a BA from the University of Michigan and a MFA from Brooklyn College. He created and edited thirteen issues of SPAWN (Sunset Park Art & Writing Newsletter) before cofounding UpSet Press with Zohra Saed. This is his first book of poems.

Cover art by Alexandra Compain-Tissier / alexandracompaintissier.com
Book design by Wendy Lee / wendyleedesign.com

Library of Congress Control Number: 2015913332

ISBN 9781937357962
Printed in the United States of America

CONTENTS

1

There are four fears: 1) the able: to be able, 2) the want—
who want, 3) the eye—to kill, 4) the ear—listen: Like the
blind, like blind people, like the congenitally deformed,
this is my private space, this is my only space is an
exception. You expect to do what you want. You expect to
do whatever you want to do & not only do you expect it,
You expect everyone besides, everyone who loves you, to
make it easy, to make it new.

—Bernadette Mayer, *Studying Hunger*

The Child, from the Ocean, Emerges

Today, more beautiful than the ocean:
the sky at night lit by fireflies.

Today, more beautiful than K: K writing
K [heart] R in the wet sand.

Today, more beautiful than Nazim's poems:
his letters to Roque calling him brother.

Today, more beautiful than the blue-green ocean:
a young boy, not afraid, wading in

and the ocean careful not to scare him.

The Poetry Group

N wore dreadlocks, and represented the homeless. He protected the brain and genitalia from blunt objects. S was bald, and represented the pawns. He protected the hands and feet from fire and frostbite. J wore her hair in a ponytail, and represented the bees. She protected the heart from all needles. Z wrapped her hair in a scarf, and represented the shadows. She protected the eyes and ears that bore witness. C had a Mohawk, and represented the youth. He protected the veins and arteries from lead poisoning. D wore her hats backwards, and represented *les guérillères*. She protected the tongue from fascist generals. B dyed her hair blue, and represented the bass players. She protected the vocal chords from smoke and smog. L had a moustache, and represented the invisible. He protected the face and torso from assassins. Together they represented the word, and could not be defeated.

GREEN

R & K are sitting on a couch facing the audience.
R is wearing shorts and a t-shirt.
K is wearing a green blouse.
A ceiling fan clicks faithfully above them.
The audience lights remain on.

R: "K, I wish you were more outgoing."

K: "You'd be very jealous."

R: "K, I wish you were a writer."

K: "You'd regret it."

R: "Why?"

K: "Because I'd write about your neuroses."

K points remote at audience.
The audience lights turn off.

R: "K."

K: "What?"

R: "I'm sorry for saying those things."

K: "You hurt my feelings."

R: "What if I massage your feet?"

K: "Here."

> *K adjusts herself to put her feet on R's lap.*
> *R begins massaging her feet, calves, thighs...*

R: "You're not wearing underwear?"

> *The stage lights turn off.*
> *Actors and audience members remain in darkness*
> *with no cue to exit.*

Cyclone

In September, most flippant
God, senescent freak,
irruptive rollercoaster
of splintered wood,
bohemians from boardwalk
beseech you, "Take me, drop me!"
And you choose, "You, you, and you,
that's it—" then lightning
singes hair of those out
(circa 1991,
wild dogs howling)
for one last ride
to Brooklyn, borough of wind,
mist, and baptism.

Opening a Red Light Camera Summons

I'd like one day to publish a book of one-line poems,
The Side Effects of Slow Motion High Diving,
I could title it. But then I ask myself,
How would this be different from a single poem
printed, in small typeset, on a page,
double-sided perhaps, sans stanzas?

When I was thirteen my father taught me to drive.
He had his own rules. For red lights he'd say,
Treat them as stop signs, but be safe,
look both ways for traffic, and behind you
for the police, and look ahead too, to the next light—
it makes no sense to pass this one only to wait at the
            next one.

A Man Said to the Universe

I read Crane's poem on the train.
It's about a man who yells, "I'm here!
See me!" (It's supposed to be a statement
but really it's a question.)
And the universe ignores him.

Others read it too. We are like the man
in Crane's poem, except we yell with our eyes.
Here, see me! No, no, see me!
Over here, I'm here!
But we're invisible.

Then, a homeless man gets on,
begs for change. No one looks at him,
not even a glance. Now, in our seats,
we are like the universe: blind.

Z

In naming you friend,
firefly, poet,
woman who fell upward

like a kite, my intention
to gift you air
in the openness of a poem

born from chaos.
You hold a mirror to my art
at an angle that elevates it,

hurls it over brownstones,
bridges, oceans.
Weaving languages you

invert light, translating day
into night, and night into day.
With a single word, "tor,"

you crack the sound barrier,
and I am permanently and proudly
scarred by your voice.

Clarion

The voice weakened by struggle
whispered into my ear
the unspeakable, the word
untranslatable,
an echo of light,
a river in the sky.

> *That which is deemed unspeakable*
> *still, when uttered, is heard.*
> *That which is left untranslated*
> *still, when found, impresses.*

The intonation suggested
a way home, a lover
naked on the ledge
of a window,
a mother's lullaby
to her nursing child.

> *It is at the ledge of transparency,*
> *a windowsill, a reflection transforms*
> *into shadow, and it is at dusk*
> *a shadow forges into night.*

Emboldened by the echo
of what could've been
the organizer's chant, the poet's lyric,
the hoarse voice of a teacher,
I could no longer remain mute.
I knew then I was born to speak.

For myself, so that without saying
the words, when I spoke of how I lived,
how I struggled, I merely had to sing
the same syllable, repeatedly—ly—ly—ly

Night in Brooklyn

I hold her sleep in my arms,
blanketing her nakedness
from winter's first storm.

Life: the electricity
passing through our bodies,
fogging our breaths.

Love: her waking,
saying, "You're not asleep yet,"
gathering me in her arms.

B in Bluestockings

Tall and beautiful (the longitude and latitude)
in a disorganized bookstore, browsing as she reads—
or short and even more beautiful (curvature
amplified by compactness) inside
an exact library, reading as she browses—
author to my dreaming, my reading
all things imaginary or unreal
that contain a promise, or the potential,
vague or certain, of becoming real,
but in which the vastest trueness exists
in the potential (this Alba, this in-between state)
not the realization (a poorly disguised ending,
a death from natural causes)—
pregnant, always, by another man.

The Blues' Blues
> or, Shadow of The Blues
> or, Bastard Child Returned Home by The Blues
>> (an Elderly Couple)
> or, The Blueueueueueueueueues

At the end (posthumously defined
as the shore) of these small
(a weighted or weighed
light)
hours (impossible
to isolate

from a lineup) on march
(unfolding) the
banners (inside
an eyelid) of
martyrs (compulsive
moralists)

who (if not
stricken)
can boast (let them
boast)
of more (may they live
just once)

Original Jesus, First & Last Jesus

Jesus of Nazareth, bearded Jesus
Chaperone of my eighth grade dance, English teacher

Jesus of Palestine, black Jesus
Lifeguard to the homeless, scarecrow to seagulls

Jesus of Israel, Jewish Jesus
Zigzagging kite, reflected in the eyes of windows

Jesus of Islam, noble Jesus
Proofreader of poetry, marathon runner

Jesus of Broadway, rockstar Jesus
Voice of hurricanes, voice of hail

Jesus of the United States of America, "God bless us" Jesus
Jesus I prayed to as a child, dollar bill Jesus

Jesus of the military, private first class Jesus
Border guard Jesus, missing in action Jesus

Jesus of the wild, Tarzan Jesus
Tree swinging, stockbroker, pyramid scheme Jesus

Jesus of mercy, wafer Jesus
Toothpick between teeth, cigarette behind ear

Jesus of the lost and missing, Houdini Jesus
Street sweeper, trickster Jesus, erasing outlines of crime
        scenes

Jesus of the dashboard, bobblehead Jesus
Yes man, laughing man, rhythm and blues man

Jesus, nodding his head to the music

Positions of Love

The window may be open, screened, or
unscreened. It will frame the moon...

When the woman and man undress each other,
       it is the *revolving door.*
When the woman and man rub thighs,
       it is the *relighting of the pilot.*
When the woman rolls right
and pulls the man on top of her,
       it is the *starboard tack.*
When the woman straddles the man's face,
       it is the *vise grip.*
When the woman goes down on the man,
       it is the *vacuum that cries.*
When the woman lies on her belly
and the man straddles her bottom,
       it is the *bow and arrow.*
When the woman holds her legs above her shoulders,
       it is the *blow horn.*
When the woman kneels on her hands and knees,
       it is the *table without chairs.*
When the woman offers her backside,
       it is the *trapdoor to the basement,*
on the east coast, but on the west coast,
       the *drop ladder to the attic.*

By Reading Poets

I have become a poet
and this long nose
has cut through thick metaphor
cut through grammar
by thinking of wind
I have become a wind
of no audio
where flies fly from
sleeping face
to sleeping face from open mouth
to open mouth
where oceans rise
lukewarm lava
where the clothesline and phone line
converge an acute angle
of here and there a city and
a child's pink eye
my child's pink eye

K

When the sun goes down
over Jamaica Bay
and lights up all the clouds
pink from within
and the water is a strong blue
ice at the shore
and it's New Year's Day eve
and I'm with you
imagining
a life with you
nowhere else
is more beautiful
than here
my avocado
my pear

2

[CAVEAT EMPTOR]

Let the buyer beware. I think that I had to for a moment act as a double agent for both the filmmakers and the public. I had to warn the public that—it's like that little beep that goes through certain recorded phone messages that you hear on the radio. I thought I would make this little beep and let the man watching me know that this is not entirely devoid of the con.

—Leonard Cohen, *Ladies and Gentlemen...*
Mr. Leonard Cohen

I Think I Married a Borges

Jorge Luis Borges has a prose poem titled, "Borges and I." It begins, "The other one, Borges, is the one things happen to," and, later on, ends, "I don't know which one of us wrote this." H'm. To divide yourself in half(!), and then for each half to attain wholeness(!!), and then for the two wholes to coexist, coupled with a plain forgetfulness (sigh), well, the possibilities are limitless. The whole world could be Borgeses. For one half, things are happening: jobs, love, happiness. For the other half, there's the cinema. "Which half is more content?" Who said that? "Me, Borges." How long have you been there? "Since this morning." It was you who drank the coffee? "Yes. Did I not leave you any?"

Dance of Infidels

The first illusion is Technicolor. Inorganic and based on falsehoods, the ego dreams itself an ego, that ego then dreams itself an ego, and so on, to infinity. We see the youth of the first ego and think it innocent. The second, third, and fourth egos see the youth of the first and they covet it.

The second illusion is Surround Sound. Secular children of Muslims and Christians, they're bused to public concerts and incumbent campaign speeches. The concerts are waiting rooms for hospice. The speeches skip on their heads like rocks on a lake. We see a lake. They see an ocean.

The third illusion is Darkness. Vacant drive-ins of memory remade as visions of an afterlife displayed on a mass tombstone. The mind perceives the image in pixels then pieces it together in reverse centrifugal order. A calculator divides and subdivides the pixels then assigns them currency. We see a calculator. The calculator sees an Adonis.

THE MARRIAGE OF R & K

R is lying on a couch reading a book.
K enters flapping a piece of paper.

K: "What's this?"

R: "What?"

K: "This!"

R: "That, my avocado, is a piece of paper."

K: "No. This: 'Missing quatrain from prison holiday?'"

R: "O that. That's a poem."

K: "It's foolishness."

R: "No, it's not foolishness. It's art."

K: "Foolishness! Why are you writing about us having sex?"

R: "I'm not. I just said we had sex that week. It was our
    tenth anniversary, you know."

K: "People don't need to know that."

R: "People know we have sex. It's not a secret."

K: "But it's private."

R: "Don't be upset, please."

K crumples the page and throws it at R.

K: "Plus we didn't have sex every day!"

R retrieves the page and un-crumples it.

R: "Well, almost every day. It's the essence of the thing, not the thing itself."

K exits.

K (offstage): "Get rid of it."

R: "Good riddance."

K (offstage): "What's that?"

R: "Are you coming to the reading?"

K (offstage): "No!"

R fist-pumps air.

Of Wide Eyes

My daughter rages
against the dying light,
each night fighting sleep
the way unarmed resistance
meets the enemy,
without recourse, wailing,
flinging her body
into the tumult
of imposing darkness,
penetrating silence.

My daughter, Najla,
nightly martyred,
champion
for eternal wakefulness.

Canoeing at Night on Greenwood Lake

Those nights, adult nights
for a child, nights stolen

from sleep, from mom,
those nights my dad took us

on the lake, he'd lie down
in the canoe, head propped

by lifejackets, and smoke a joint.
My brother and I'd paddle.

"Don't make noise," he'd say
each time we banged the side.

"Pretend we're escaping prison."
And I could feel the moon

on my back like a searchlight.
I could hear the lake

quietly, secretly, breathing.
"Otters," he'd say, "your paddling

should sound like that."
And I could feel the weight

of my young arms trying
to copy the otters.

I Will Receive You

I will receive you in Greenwood Cemetery
The cemetery has no ears
We will embrace alongside the lake
The lake is blind
I will point out the informant
The informant is a hideous creature
I will introduce you to the grave robber
The grave robber you can trust

I will receive you in Timboo's
We will drink at the bar
The bar is a bookshelf you help yourself to
I will collect my winnings from the bookie
The bookie is a retired boxer
I will introduce you to the bartender
He will explain the vig
It may be different for you

I will receive you on Steeplechase Pier

The cross of Coney Island

We will smoke a joint at its tip

The tip is reserved for us

I will buy a couple of beers from the vendor

He will not sell to just anyone

I will introduce you because

You ought to be able to buy beers yourself

I will receive you on the corner

Of Smith and Pacific

The corner is our boardroom

We will negotiate there

I will do all the talking

You will simply listen

If I introduce you

Just nod your head—got it?

To Hear Z / To Hear N

When you hear Z read it's like watching a tightrope walker walk across town on the clotheslines of immigrants. A moment ago you may have been at a reading but now you're standing on a rooftop. There were others when you arrived but they have since disappeared. Z is reading a poem about exile, and burying umbilical cords, and a train ride over the Manhattan Bridge, and you're seeing these things as if looking out the train window. Her scarf is a cape that gives her power. Like Wonder Woman's lasso, she can tie you up and make you tell the truth. As you tell it she is whispering it back in your ear.

When you hear N read it's like walking into a crowded bar from a side street where a queue of smoke is waiting for you like a string of ex-wives. In the back corner, with a pint of stout in one hand and a dart in the other, is N aiming his story of how, on the same day, without showering in-between, he made love to two women, mixing their fragrances like a drink. You may have arrived sober but now you're inebriated. He has you on stage telling stories you shouldn't. Once you tell them they no longer belong to you, they become free. But before they are free, they are his for the night.

R

I was born from a conversation omitted from a screenplay written by language poets. At an impressionable age I ran away from home. I joined up with Roque Dalton and Nazim Hikmet. They were satirical sharpshooters, but poor guardians, always in and out of jail, or in hiding. I returned home an orphan of politics. Alone in the wilderness of the city, on the verge of drowning, I was rescued by surrealists in the form of a school of hammerhead sharks. They carried me to the shore of Coney Island, where I met my wife. We played happily in the sand, but she refused to sleep under the stars. She brought me home with her and gave me two beautiful poems. I'll always love these two beautiful poems. Still she wouldn't sleep under the stars. Then I met Paul Celan and Anne Sexton. They got along famously. They asked me to join their poetry group. I said yes. We met regularly at a café that had outdoor seating. H.D. was our hostess. I stayed up nights dreaming about a *ménage à quatre*. Routinely my wife took my two beautiful poems to bed with her. They became her poems. I asked for them back. She said no, I'd have to write new poems. I said I can't write new poems by myself. She said too bad, call your poetry group. She was expert at mocking me. Screw the group, I lied. This pleased her. I took a break from the group. This pleased her further. Then Anne called, she said Paul was a jerk, could I meet her?

This Alba Does Exist

This Alba split the fog of my brain
This Alba glows in the dark of my eardrum
This Alba, a thousand umbrellas opening
This Alba I thought inanimate rising
from subway grates, steaming my pores
This Alba, the city, on its hind legs
poised to leap This Alba, a counterbalance
handcuffed to a high wire act This Alba,
inverting our bodies, in free fall
This Alba, a blank page, a clean backside
This Alba absconded with the hostage
This hostage

Driftings

Last night I dreamt a hundred dreams and you were in each one. In one you were very tired and pregnant, and fell asleep, so I carried you, as if we were newly married, around the city looking for spumoni. I was to wake you if I found pistachio. Even pregnant you were incredibly light, no heavier than an open loose-leaf binder. In another I was trying to tell you I love you but you didn't believe me. You insisted I was joking or exaggerating. Trying to convince you was quite frustrating. In another more intimate one, I was laying you on the foot of your bed crosswise when your roommate surprised us. I didn't know you had a roommate but it seemed natural that you did. He had a schoolbag that I inspected and it was completely empty but he carried it on his back from one dream to the next. In most of the dreams you were sleeping and were made even more beautiful by sleep. I realized I had never before seen you asleep, and to now have your sleeping image before me, even in a dream state, made me grateful, content. The feeling was so pure I couldn't bear it and I had to step out for some air. I was careful not to wake you. I went out to sit on your stoop. There was a guy there who knew everything about your street, a side street in the city somewhere, and everyone who lived there. He was excited to talk to me and took me by the hand to give me a tour of your neighbors' homes. Upon entering the first one, we were in a church, and all your neighbors were there too. He would introduce me to them and they would say, "Peace be with you," and I would respond, "Thanks." The exchange was awkward but not at all rude. I snuck out through the bathroom window and renewed my search for spumoni, this time alone. While I was walking around, the city would morph under my feet: a dead-end street would open onto a busy intersection; a row of residential houses would turn into stores overflowing with merchandise; cars in the street floated up like boats on a river; a bridge was being erected, as if being drawn into a cartoon, over my head; and what was once day was suddenly night and then vice versa and then alternating, creating a gargantuan strobe effect. I returned to you sleeping on the foot of your bed. You were on your side now, in the fetal position, and your child too, I imagined inside you, in the same position, like those Russian dolls made up of smaller dolls. I started kissing you, small innocent pecks on your bare legs. My odd kisses erased your birthmarks. My even ones replaced them.

Self Portrait as Starfish

I stare at the surface
a ceiling shadows alight
on cloudy wobbling
buoys' swiveling lights
disjointed flashes of
high beams and brake lights
I suspect the moon
under cover of ambulatory lights
of molesting my eyes
the fog's embryo a lightless
freeway of overtaking
my ache for northern lights
the sea foam of a silent film
pimping my nightlight for a bag of weed

Jamaica: A Homecoming

I've dawned, another
sweet and strange, slippery
kiss on my skin, dragon

lips, Roman numeral, enamel
lips, torsos, thighs, calves
tied, two silk sleeves, dolphin-smooth

almost human, I feel inside a knot
I open with my fingers
in, out of water

foam, form
nude sculptures of
an underwater city, ancient

land, indrawn
drawn into deep abyss
of blue coral

an island, inhabited
by such sculptures, alive
radiant, procreating

muteness, sketched before drawn
this place seen
no more outside dream

in pale, uncertain
light—
then birdsong (hummingbirds)

I've dawned, no more twilight
no more, today, her dissimilar
shade of haze, shade of whiteness

First Writing Since

First writing since I broke my neck
I was not paralyzed
instead my arms and legs tingle
my top lip buzzes I feel like
I have a moustache except I have no moustache

First writing since I watched *La Moustache*
a French film the saddest film ever
I thought I was renting a comedy
a guy shaves his moustache and
no one recognizes him ha ha but no
I was wrong a guy shaves his moustache and
no one remembers his moustache
not even (especially) his wife

First writing since I cried
after watching *La Moustache*
it felt like I came
for the first time ever
I didn't even cry when I broke my neck
I tried to but
I wasn't paralyzed

The Waiter

I'm at the table waiting for my wife
to return from the restroom.

I drink my wine and I drink her wine too.
Our waiter is also missing, I notice

because of the empty wine glasses.
When she returns, she returns sweating.

"Are you sweating?" I ask her.
"No," she says, "I splashed water on my face."

"What is that smell?" I say.
"What smell?" she says.

"That smell, like sex," I say.
"How would you know?" she says.

"Ha, very funny," I say.
"No, not really," she says, "very sad."

"Yeah, very sad," I say, "sad as lowercase f."
"What?" she says.

"You slept with that waiter," I say.
"So," she says.

A HECKLER'S TRIUMPH

*A heckler walks up to a podium and rotates it 180
degrees.*
*With his back to the audience, he begins reading
mockingly...*

Heckler: "I see myself in degrees of days since I last shaved,
and what I'm reading at the time. In Jamaica I was
reading Bernadette Mayer, and went ten days without
shaving, zero without sex."

A second heckler interrupts, yells out.

2nd Heckler: "Teach me! Teach me! Over here."

The original heckler turns around.

Heckler: "'Teach you?' Teach you what? Good manners?
Lord knows you have none."

2nd Heckler: "No. No. Teach me to write. Like you."

Chorus (a select few from audience): "Yeah man, teach
him..."

Heckler: "If you want to write, read."

Chorus (hereon the whole audience): "Boooooo..."

2nd Heckler: "I don't want to read. I want to be a poet!"

Applause.

Heckler: "'To be a poet?' Ha! You?! To be a poet, you must make poet-friends."

2nd Heckler: "'Poet-friends?'"

Heckler: "Yes, they will teach you."

2nd Heckler: "But where? Where are they? How do I meet them?"

Chorus: "Yeah, where? Show us. We don't see any!"

Heckler: "They're in coffee shops. Like this one, only nicer."

2nd Heckler: "But I don't drink coffee."

Chorus: "Coffee sucks! Fuck Starbucks!"

Heckler: "Then, they're in bars. They love beer."

Applause.

2nd Heckler: "But I hate beer. I can't stand its taste."

Chorus: "Boooooo…"

Heckler: "Then, they're in college. They teach composition."

2nd Heckler: "But I can't get into college, my grades are too low."

    Applause.

Heckler: "Then, I don't know what to tell you. You cannot meet them."

3

I KNOW OF A PLACE BETWEEN BETWEEN, BEHIND BEHIND, IN FRONT OF FRONT, BELOW BELOW, ABOVE ABOVE, INSIDE INSIDE, OUTSIDE OUTSIDE, CLOSE TO CLOSE, FAR FROM FAR, MUCH FARTHER THAN FAR, MUCH CLOSER THAN CLOSE, ANOTHER SIDE OF ANOTHER SIDE...

—Bob Kaufman, *All Hallows, Jack O'Lantern Weather,*
North of Time

The Marriage of R & K

K loves and hates R.
Her hate doesn't dilute her love.
R loved then hated K and now
loves her again. However
his love is a shotgun.

K cannot separate her feelings.
As she forgives, she withdraws
her forgiveness. R senses this
back and forth, and sees behind it
a half-god becoming a demon, then
   a martyr.

The Poetry Group Tombstone

First came N and Z trading kisses on paper, slipping them inside the folds of fat they hid from their people's hunger. From this secret fondling came R and L. R wearing the umbilical cord of his newborn son, peeling off his wife's handprints. L smelling like a broken curfew, sculpting incense smoke into the face of his father. Then D, with her hat on backwards and her bag of sugar for the flies, writing poems with her needle-pricked fingers. Then J, bringing a basket of ovaries for the group to munch on, laughing at the poems our poems wanted to be. Then, sadly, L disappeared, called away by a woman wearing the mask of his mother. He was missed. In his place came S, husband of D, barking at the edges of her poems, putting the group on his chessboard and playing for beers. His music growing in her belly. Then there was C who came and went, circling the group, his Mohawk a shark fin, leaving behind the chum of ex-girlfriends. Then N brought in Q in a failed attempt to sleep with her. She left an outline for the men to fill with side-glances. Then N met B at Bluestockings, and there is a picture to prove this. She undressed and re-dressed the group, measuring our waistlines for the season finale. But the newborns ate our poetry, and there was nothing left to say that could be said in front of the children. All that was left was N and R sharing coffee on a cum-stained couch lamenting those seeds, because a poem dies but a child lasts forever.

SAND

R and K are in a beachfront restaurant at a resort.

The stage splits R and K, and the table between them, and rotates them each 90 degrees (R clockwise, K counterclockwise) so that they are both facing the audience.

When they talk, they talk directly to the audience.

Behind R is the ocean, waveless, and a few fishing boats anchored offshore.

Behind K is the commotion of the restaurant and its guests.

R: "I feel sorry for the people working here. They probably make next to nothing."

K: "At least they have a job."

R: "A job? They have to bend over backwards for a bunch of idiots on vacation who expect them to bend over backwards for them and treat them like royalty. It's not a job. It's a punishment."

K: "You're one of the idiots. You don't understand what it is to have nothing and to have to choose between working and not working, and make sacrifices to put food on the table. They don't get to choose between cushiony jobs. Their choice is work, or no work."

R: "Bullshit. Yes, I'm one of the idiots. But bullshit I don't understand what it is to make sacrifices. I've had some real shitty jobs in my life too. At some point, in those jobs, you realize, it's better not to work, that that's the better, long-term choice. The idea that you should feel grateful for a job, any job, is the scam. The more you think that, believe that, the longer you'll stay at your shitty job and be taken advantage of."

K: "You're so spoiled and used to your parents helping you out that you don't realize not everyone can walk away from their job. I'm not saying it's right that they get paid so little and have to put up with so much, but it's still better than starving."

R: "Oh my god. You're so melodramatic. Quitting doesn't equal starvation. Come on, the choice is not 'quit and starve,' or 'work and live.'"

K: "Not in your world, no. But here, yes. That's the choice, believe me I know. I'm from here. Remember?"

R: "Yes, I remember. I rescued you from all this."

K: "You did not rescue me. I didn't need you for anything, and I still don't. I can't believe you said that. You should really think before you talk. And sometimes, honestly, I wish I was still here, with my mother."

R: "Then you should ask for an application. Maybe they're hiring."

K gets up to walk away.

R: "Wait. Do you hear that?"

K: "What?"

R: "Bob Marley, again. It's every day, all day. Like elevator music. This is the greatest artist of all time and they've reduced him, his legacy, to background dining music. It makes me nauseous."

K: "You make me nauseous."

K walks away.
R sips his coffee, looks after her, then behind him, at the ocean.
Bob Marley's "Redemption Song" playing in the background.

Poetry (& Poets) vs. Not-Poetry

I have thirteen bookcases
I divided into two teams.
The first team I labeled
"Poetry (& Poets)."
On this team I include
biographies of poets,
prose works by poets,
Zora Neale Hurston
and Henry Miller.
The second team I labeled
"Not-Poetry."
I hide my porn
in these bookcases.

Note on Subway Seat
or, How I Contracted Herpes

A curse on the husband who cheats
A curse on his necktie
A curse on his checking account
A curse on his genitals
A curse on his soft hands
A curse on his deep-tissue sports-massage
A curse on his attorney-client privilege
A curse on his Sunday mornings

> The train emerged onto the bridge
> The sun was shining while it was raining

A curse on the American dream

> The train got stuck
> All the people looked up from their magazines

A curse on the comeback story

> A homeless man with no legs entered the car

A curse on People's fifty most beautiful people

> He walked on his hands with a sign that read
> "Veteran"

A curse on excess adorations of all things military

All the people looked down at their magazines

A curse on caring about anyone

I looked down too

A curse on once upon a time

The man passed through the car

A curse on happily ever after
A curse on Atlantic City
A curse on New Year's Eve
A curse on new Times Square
A curse on new Yankee Stadium
A curse on new New York
A curse on you too
A curse on your genitals

The train jerked forward

Elegy for N

When his unofficial ex-wife reentered his life, neither sun nor moon shone on the ceiling of his sleep. He was helpless, lost, fumbling in the dark alleys of his dreams. He felt her hand on his chest, pressing. He imagined the handprint it would leave. Surely, he thought, it would glow red. It would brand him, as hers, for a second time. A new tattoo over an old one: a cover-up, a mask. Or maybe: a rebirth, a reclamation. He wasn't certain. She whispered something in his ear. Her breath smelled like the insides of a church. All his senses, it seemed, suddenly had a superhero's receptivity. He was asleep, weightless, flying over lakes of lava, acutely aware she was controlling him as if in a video game. But he couldn't wake up, and not from lack of effort. It was simply impossible. He was back in her grip, resuscitated and exhausted, stuck inside her first mix tape: Depeche Mode's "Somebody" twenty times in a row, back-to-back-to-back. She was taking him back to her lair. She was going to have her way with him. Only afterward, after the child would be born, would she allow him to wake up and live: a father first, a husband in name alone.

Four Pillars of Morn

1.

we holding up this globe
four hundred thousand times
our combined size, a topless
volume, an Alaska of daylight
as rainbow, as boomerang

we north, west, south, east
two brothers, two sisters
columns of ozone, trees
weary and slumping, the
weight of sun on our necks

2.

we north, west, south, east
four hundred thousand times

as rainbow, as boomerang
weary and slumping, the

columns of ozone, trees
our combined size, a topless

weight of sun on our necks
volume, an Alaska of daylight

two brothers, two sisters
we holding up this globe

3.

we holding up this globe
two brothers, two sisters
our combined size, a topless
weary and slumping, the
as rainbow, as boomerang

weight of sun on our necks
volume, an Alaska of daylight
columns of ozone, trees
four hundred thousand times
we north, west, south, east

4.

we north, west, south, east
we holding up this globe

four hundred thousand times
two brothers, two sisters

columns of ozone, trees
our combined size, a topless

volume, an Alaska of daylight
weary and slumping, the

weight of sun on our necks
as rainbow, as boomerang

Night in Manhattan

Your voice fills my ear like pool water.
I cannot shake it loose.

On your roof, a fog settles,
dissolving the city below.

Weightlessly, you pull yourself up
on the ledge, cross your legs, dangle

your sandals from your toes.
I lean toward you, free of fear.

What secrets there are between us
we haven't kept from each other.

What secrets there are before us,
looking down, we hesitate to dare.

When we kiss, I imagine our poems
sharing a page in a journal.

B

I have a crush on B.
She's so sexy and upright.
I look up and I see her multiplied
in the windows of skyscrapers. I close my eyes
and I hear her whispering directions,
"This way west." I follow
her voice. It's smoke.
It's liquid.
It's the silk wings
of twirling batons. It floods
the amphitheaters of my eye sockets,
my nostrils. I want to somersault, cartwheel,
and backflip on the mat of her tongue. I want to dive
inside her lung. I want to snuggle against
the wall of her bladder, tickle her
until she has to pee.

> *B, my hot-air balloon*
> *of bombazine, my boat*
> *of sweet basil, my Bolero*
> *partner, buddleia*
> *of my balcony, Juneberry*
> *of my neighbor's backyard, bandolier*
> *of my rescue buoy, deep blue*
> *current of my bobbing—*

"B, take me with you, please."

A Prison Holiday

I have looked into mirrors
and my face has looked back
the face of another man
from another country
a country of many dialects
where I loved too many too often
but none loved me back
except you *Face That Looks Back*
you don't have to smile to smile
you laugh to laugh (for me that's enough)

Love Letters to Marcus Garvey

I fear you, Marcus Garvey, I fear your legacy, your black children, all the secrets I've told you, I can see them published in future newspapers, obituaries for each betrayal, a race of little monsters

I hate you, Marcus Garvey, I hate your blackness, how it shines on stage, your voice crawling over the heads of a mixed audience, black smoke snaking its way through the aisles, flashlight in its mouth, hunting for hypocrites

I miss you, Marcus Garvey, I miss your speeches, nighttime under a streetlight, in print in *Negro World*, in bed practicing on me, shadows and darkness alternating with each passing car, your intelligent eyes would make my husband self-combust

I need you, Marcus Garvey, to stay in the city, not to move to Panama, or London, I know it's heartless here, and the trees are crucifixes, but the people, when they cry out, they want to be recorded, they expect jazz

I name you, Marcus Garvey, Black Man of wind gusts, categories one, two and three, Benedict Arnold of falling trees, behemoth oaks, flying debris as St. Johns the Baptists, Hitler of floods, I can defend you, I can embrace drowning

I seek you, Marcus Garvey, in the spots on my skin, these are my gods, my cancers, not the people's political party you envisioned, huh, multiple gods, multiple aims, multiple destinies competing for custody of one sun

I hide you, Marcus Garvey, I pretend you don't exist, I pretend you're white, an iceberg, black at the core then graying outward to a snowy skin, a leather jacket with fur lining, I put you on and flip your collar up to my ears, I have no feeling in my hands, you have no pockets

I hear you, Marcus Garvey, in the headlines I read, in the engine rooms of modern-day slave ships, in the living rooms of Harlem, as a cat in the asylum of a fire escape, breaking up with your white mistresses in the backseats of cabs

I kill you, Marcus Garvey, I have killed you before, and you have come back to life, but this time is different, because while I am killing you I am unbuttoning my blouse to the Ku Klux Klan, I am parting your seed

I am you, Marcus Garvey, today I survived my second stroke, unlike you, I have almost no voice left, but I have an empty grave with my name on it, I have a daughter, and a guitar, a desert and a horizon I call mulatto

Water

A person is all water. A geyser
takes shape and walks off,
learns how to speak,
cry, laugh,

tastes air once
and doesn't want to go back
to her or his hole,
a heavy dose of darkness.

It's better in the shadows
of earth's curvature
to show some cleavage
and feel the wind between one's legs.

There's a city of lights
in a wet kiss, an ocean
blinking on and off
waiting for

a type of water
that swims in water
and another type of water
that harvests it.

Woman, Man (O My Friends)

Woman. Man.
Child is both
at play
alone, playing
against oneself,
tug of war, cops,
robbers, fighting,
fleeing.
       Fireflies:
Agnes and her daughter,
Alex and her son.

Woman. Man.
Mother, father,
is neither
in fog of God or
like God,
like fog, skyward,
inward, looking down,
up, unsure.
       Samba, semba:
the clouds' soundless
blue-black baby-making.

Woman. Man.
Illustration, a line
curved
or looped, or straight,
rooted in lines,
sailing ahead,
a jib, swollen,
its shape its sex,
          powered by wind. My friends:
falling coral offspring,
infant tsunamis.

Up Prospect Hill

To wake up inside a closed pullout couch

To cross the Belt Parkway on foot backwards perhaps
even moonwalking

To attempt suicide by jumping off a bridge when it's nice
out and not a very high bridge

To be crazy in a time when there are more crazy houses
than crazies

To not make sense by accident and then claim to not
have made sense on purpose

To define surreal as a latte with skim milk instead of
whole milk

To walk your bike through a construction site that was
once a street you could ride your bike on drunk
or not

To ask your wife to pretend she's your sister just this one
time

To sprinkle sugar over your diabetic coworker's artificially
sweetened retirement cake

To know when enough is enough and too little is also
enough in other words to know when change is
required

To write your way to divorce then the children can read
about it when they get older and maybe take
your side

To stay up all night watching CSI reruns and sleep
     routinely punching you in your side
To give up now or to give up later because to not give up
     simply means to give up later when nobody's
     looking
To lie to yourself which is not really lying because duh
     you know the truth
To lie to someone else though it's like hitting a walk-off
     single to win the World Series (later officially
     scored an error)

LOVE POEM FOR R

R and K are on a train.
The train is crowded and neither one has a seat
     at first but then a nice man gets up to give his
     seat to K.
K is seven months pregnant.
The nice man is an actor hired for the role.
R takes out a notebook and begins writing in it.
He writes "Love Poem for R" on top of a blank
     page.
As he writes, what he writes is communicated to
     the audience through the subway ticker.
He hands the notebook to K.
She sucks her teeth, "Cho!"

K: "No sir."

R: "Please."

K: "No, I can't."

R: "Yes, you can."

K: "No. I don't know how."

R: "I'm begging."

K: "No."

R: "Please. Come on."

K: "No."

R: "It's easy. Just break up your thoughts into lines, that's all."

K writes.

The subway ticker: *I love you. I love you. I love you. Happy???*

4

And now, we have no option. We can't say *maybe, it's possible, it looks very probable...* No way! We have to say this is what the Bible teaches! This is fact! May 21, 2011 is the day of the Rapture. It is the day that Judgment Day begins...

—Harold Camping, *Topics from the Open Forum*

Remembering Wong Kee

Ah Robert
If I gave you a divorce
What would you do with it

> *I'd take a one-bedroom*
> *No TV, no phone*
> *Just a desk and computer, no internet*

But Robert
If I gave you a divorce
What about the children

> *Yes, the children love me*
> *They'd cry for days*
> *I'd cry for years*

Ah Robert
What if, instead of a divorce
I died, making you a widower

> *I'd kill myself too*
> *Knowing your death was no accident*
> *The children would be orphaned*

But Robert

If I gave you a divorce

Would you be happy

Do you remember our first date

Wong Kee

It doesn't exist anymore

The Poetry Group Grope

Thus Z grafted on N, freeness, N grafted on R, faith, R grafted on L, God, L grafted on J, a picture of his heart with all our hearts inside it, J grafted on D, our prayers, the poems we read to each other, D grafted on S, life force, S grafted on B, deep, deep breathing, B grafted on C, the orgasm, and C (his green eyes) grafted on the orgasm the letters p and x and the number 1, a double fisherman's knot, two half-hitches, two round turns and a half-hitch, an overhand knot and a bowline, then we all rolled our own cigarettes

THE PIER

R and K are on a beach watching the sunset.
K begins writing in the sand.
There is a pool situated between the audience and
the stage.
Inside the pool there is a child in waist-high water.

R: "K."

K: "Yes."

R: "I know what I want."

K: "What?"

R: "For you to have the baby."

K: "You mean *for us?*"

R: "Yes, *for us* to have the baby."

R & K embrace.
The child dives into the water and remains
submerged.

A Shooting in the Country

There's a walk-bridge, wide
enough for one person to cross, with
a leaning, makeshift roof of leafage. I'm
on one side of the bridge with the tourists. The locals
are on the other side. I can see them
through the bridge. The tourists devise
a game. One takes a target, a piece of debris,
or bark, across the bridge and stands at the foot
of the other side holding it in front of his chest.
His buddy takes aim with a rifle and shoots
the target. Then they switch roles. I watch
several shootings. My daughter volunteers
to take a target across the bridge. The locals
embrace her. They give her a new target. I'm
handed a rifle. I study the target's outline.
I take a deep breath and shoot. My daughter,
frantic, gives back the target then runs
towards me. I look past her. There's
a man. He's holding it up to the sky, wailing.

Despair/the Rapture: The Rise & Fall of Harold Camping

There are lies above despair.
There are lies that smell of mold.
There are lies that have strong alibis.
There are lies that sound like promises.
There are lies that are gold-plated.
There are lies that have the static of an a.m. dial.
There are lies that subsume an applause machine.

Dabbed with peroxide,
there are lies that mutate.
There are lies that insulate the immune system.
Some too atomic to see with the naked eye,
lies that run along galactic floorboards.
Daily, there are lies
that abduct the clerics of paradise.

Today, for instance, there are lies
retreating westward,
on a turbulent flight,
harnessed to their chairs.

The Devil

I'd like to move in with him, just temporarily.
We'd have great conversations about God and art and
        women.

He wouldn't keep track of my comings and goings.
I could stay out all night drinking or playing poker.
        He wouldn't lock me out.

I could date his sister or cousin or ex-girlfriend.
        He wouldn't mind.
We'd combine our books, my bookshelves and his milk
        crates,

leave our unfinished poems around, taped to walls,
        as bookmarkers or coasters,
and write in the margins, between stanzas, our
        comments and revisions.

If I'd dedicate a poem to my wife, he'd cross out the
        dedication or change her name to a famous
        porn star.
Sometimes he'd make me laugh so hard I'd have an
        asthma attack.

We wouldn't hide our porn collections, except when our
         mothers visited, or my children, or the once-was
         poetry group.
On most nights, we'd sit in front of the fire (his place has
         a fireplace),

read poems, tell jokes, drink hot chocolate, then what
         gets me in trouble
every time, smoke weed, write a collaborative dirge, go
         on craigslist, reenact Burning Man.

A Little Poem for the Revolution

In Florida, the cars
are the people, and the people
are the car batteries.

Do not mourn the car batteries!

In New York City, the people are actors
playing people, and the cars are luxury
mobile telephone booths.

Do not applaud the actors!

In the Future, the people are restored
as victims, and the cars are three- and four-legged
zombies plowing, plowing, plowing.

Do not indict the zombies!

If an Empty Seaport

You chart my shy grammar.
(No one else does that.)

We squabble to flirt.
(Lorca or Borges?)

At Schaefer Landing
I lift up your skirt.

If an empty seaport on a winter night.
(My heart flutters.)

I whisper, *Beautiful.*
Legions of smiley faces bob in the river,

an audience for our film.
(Rated R. NC-17, Director's cut.)

I want to exchange my passport for your passport.
(Do you think they would object?)

Night of Always

I startle myself awake from a nightmare
I'm in the night of always
I break my neck bodysurfing at night
I'm in the night of always
I visit four prostitutes in one night
I'm in the night of always
I laugh out loud
Others laugh at me for my outburst
The night of always laughs at me too
The night of always has outdrank me again
Unfazed I hold a candle to my face and squint my eyes
I can see through the night of always
He's an impostor I mean he's really a she
I get in my car
There's a sticky note on the steering wheel
It says "sbf"
I drive into the night of always
I don't get far
The note upside down says "gas"
I suspect the night of always
I break into the local community college
I carry my bike up to the third floor and ride it through the
        hallways
As I ride the motion sensor lights flick on behind me
I'm the new dean of the new college of the new night of
        always

The newly lit hallways appear funereal in my wake

I find a run-down marina

I climb to the roof of a fishing boat and wrap myself in its
        tarp

It's the tarp of the night of always

I can see my distorted reflection

In its metallic gears

I see a man with facial hair and no memory of a smile

Pi

I see a long narrow hallway

I see a door at the end

I see a nameplate on the door

It says "The Reading"

I open the door

It's a waiting room

There are three other men

They look like me

One has a moustache (he is in a wheelchair)

One is a statue (no arms)

One has a mullet (sleeveless shirt)

I'm in the doorway

The moustache has a tape recorder in his lap

The statue is wearing a headset microphone

The mullet is twirling a kitchen timer

I fumble through my pockets

I find a quarter

We stare silently

Then the statue says

"I see a long narrow hallway"

Sadness

Sadness takes off her make-up
and puts on her Jerusalem—takes off her Jerusalem
and puts on her make-up—treading water

as squid circle her
as sharks circle the squid
as giant groupers circle the sharks

in an encrypted backchannel
a man and a woman
a literature professor and a marine biologist

choreograph the courtship—typing
between bites we are ripples
or are we talking two women here

or are we talking two men
either way I am drunk
your drunkenness is not a cathedral

no it's a warning
I am taking off my make-up
I am putting on my Jerusalem

K

If this then that, if that then this, so it is with K, judge of my being, wife of my days, measuring my love like the pH level of a pool. If only I could convince her, crystal of my want, I love her, she wouldn't have to ask me, test me, grade me like one of her students, nor run away hoping I run after her. She'd know I'm hers, and in that knowing she'd trust I'd return. If that were enough, then we could base jump off the Verrazano with one parachute between us, not strapped to either of us, and complete confidence in our landing safe, atop the orchestra of our doubters. If this was our starting point, our home base, we could be homeless and have everything, make ourselves invisible, spy on our fears without fear, be happy the way a wild animal is wild, an eye open, blinking. Oh, if I could put all my longing into a single kiss and kiss her between her legs. The dome of night would break like a windshield, the whole planet inside this egg, this cockpit, cracking, one crack at first, then splintering out in different directions, like lightning, captured as in a photo, veins glowing under skin. From this egg, our two children would be born: one, of wide eyes; the other, listening.

The Live Dissection of R (as Performed by The Poetry Group)

The Poetry Group adorned their protective goggles and rubber gloves. R tilted his head up from the operating table and smiled at the witnesses. His wife and children elected not to attend. Instead, all the women he slept with were there. It was a small room of vowels, sighs, and yawns. N narrated the dissection, naming each part he lifted from the table.

"The first part, the upper left vertical line, is known as The Grip. It anchors the second part, the loop line, which I refer to as a backwards c, otherwise known as The Boomerang. These two parts, when joined, comprise the top. The third part, the lower left vertical line, is known as The Pillar. It adjoins the fourth and final part, a 45-degree angled sloping line, I have pegged The Slide. The clinical term, I believe, is The Normal Male Pee Trajectory. These two parts, when joined, comprise the bottom. It is important to distinguish the top from the bottom. Now, before we attempt to reassemble R, are there any questions?"

"Yes. Do you have to reassemble him?"

Within a Night: Four Nights

The first night, night in Brooklyn:
lovers confront a concourse of thieves.

The second night, nadir of non-guilt:
pleas of Mayday muffled by pre-recorded applause.

The third night, bridge leading into fog:
ghosts of jumpers retrace their falling.

The fourth night, unending hour of hazards:
the con, ladies and gentlemen, is not devoid of truth.

About the Author

I'm a poet. However,
I don't write poems,
I compose them. Still,
I'm less a composer than
I am a poet. And
I'm less a poet than
I am a mathematician. And
I'm less a mathematician than
I am someone who loves math:
the chameleon.

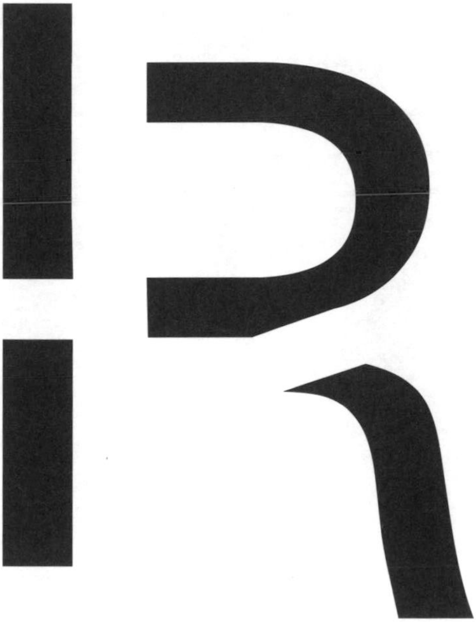

ACKNOWLEDGMENTS

I'm grateful to so many for their input and support. I'm especially indebted to my wife, my family & friends, my teachers, The Poetry Group, and my readers: Zohra Saed, Nicholas Powers, Karen Pittelman, Matthew Rotando, and Matthew Burgess. I'd also like to thank the editors of *Mizna* and *Brooklyn Review*, where a couple of these poems first appeared.

Montreal: Requiem for the Tittle

I'm walking in darkness
        on gravel and
I'm worried about my ankle

I see oversized
        silhouettes move and
bend towards me

trees as traffic lights
        branchless
bobbing "as if floating"

all the middle lights
        "what should be yellow"
blinking black

dream-buoys
        a wind is carrying "and"
and I'm walking into this wind

nervous "to exploit"
        an illicit act
a dream-fiend from the future

my victim's mind
        masturbating in a pool
I listen for mercy

I hear my pre-cum "its lightness"
        an unintended humming
I see behind me

far back
        blurred "a light"
shrinking and flashing

then nothing
        "an asterisk" darkness
surrounding a smaller farther light